NATIONAL
GEOGRAPHIC

T0080632

Ladders

PATTERNS

Passage of Time

by Rebecca L. Johnson

Long before there were clocks, watches, and smart phones, people used the sun, moon, and stars to track the passage of time. The sun was the most obvious natural time-keeper. The sun follows a predictable, daily pattern. It appears to rise in the east and appears to move across the sky until it sets in the west. As the sun appears to move in the sky, shadows cast by trees, rocks, and other objects change location on the ground. Early humans learned to judge the approximate time of day by the sun's position overhead and the length and position of shadows on the ground.

Obelisks

The ancient Egyptians were one of the first cultures to use special shadow-casting objects to help tell time more precisely. The Egyptians erected tall, four-sided stone monuments called **obelisks** to honor their sun god. Obelisks also cast very long shadows and so worked as a sort of clock. How? The Egyptians placed markers around the bottom of some obelisks. The markers represented divisions of time during the day—something like our hours. As the sun appeared to travel across the sky, an obelisk's shadow would move from marker to marker. At a glance, Egyptians could see the shadow's position and know what time it was.

⌃ Ancient Egyptians built this obelisk. It was used to tell time.

Sundials

Most Egyptian obelisks were huge, single blocks of stone that weighed many tons. They were definitely not portable! Ancient people saw a need for smaller, more practical time-keeping devices. **Sundials** were one answer.

Like an obelisk, a sundial uses a moving shadow to mark the passage of time. A sundial has a small projecting stick, called a gnomon (ˈnō-mən), which casts a shadow on a surface marked with lines.

The lines represent divisions of time, much like the numbers on the face of a clock. As the sun appears to move overhead, the shadow of the gnomon moves from line to line, indicating the time.

Some sundials were flat while others were curved like a bowl. At the Imperial Palace in Beijing, China, there is an ancient carved stone sundial—called a "rigui" in Chinese—shaped like a tilted disc or wheel. The metal gnomon is positioned in the center of the rigui, casting a shadow on the stone surface.

∧ This sundial is located at the Imperial Palace in Bejing, China.

Stone Circles

Ancient civilizations also tracked the seasons. Some did this by marking the sun's position at different times of year with the help of stone circles.

Stonehenge is a large stone circle complex in southern England. Massive stone blocks, set upright like pillars, form a large outer circle and a smaller inner circle. Other stones lie atop some of the upright stones. Archaeologists, scientists who study ancient civilizations, think Stonehenge was built over many centuries,

∧ The shape of Stonehenge can best be seen from above.

beginning about 3100 B.C. Prehistoric people may have gathered at Stonehenge to remember their ancestors and bury their dead. From inside the stone circle, they also observed—and celebrated— important sun-related events during the year.

Solstices were two of these events. The summer solstice is the day with the most daylight hours and marks the beginning of summer in the northern hemisphere. On the summer solstice, the rising sun aligns perfectly between two of Stonehenge's enormous stone pillars. The winter solstice is the day with the least number of daylight hours and marks the beginning of winter in the northern hemisphere. On the winter solstice, the setting sun lines up precisely between another set of stones at Stonehenge.

This is how Stonehenge may have looked after the stones were first put into place

The Mayan Calendar

Most ancient civilizations gradually developed calendars to keep track of days, months, and years. The ancient Maya of Central America noticed patterns in how the sun, moon, and stars seemed to move and change in the sky. Combining this knowledge with mathematics, they created a number of different calendars. One calendar was the Haab'.

The Haab' is a yearly calendar with 365 solar days grouped into 18 months of 20 days each and one month which is only 5 days long. The calendar has an outer ring of Mayan glyphs (pictures) which represent each of the 19 months. Each day is represented by a number in the month followed by the name of the month. Each glyph represents a personality associated with the month.

Ancient Haab' calendars are usually carved circles in stone. Each carved character represents part of a 365-day year.

The life of the ancient Maya revolved around the concept of time. Mayan priests were consulted on civil, agricultural and religious matters. The Haab' was the calendar they used to plan important seasonal activities, such as planting seeds and harvesting crops. Time was of such importance that children were even named after the date on which they were born. However, the ancient Maya also thought the five days at the year's end were unlucky, a time when evil spirits caused trouble.

The Roman Calendar

Half a world away from the Maya, in Europe, the ancient Romans came up with a different calendar. It combined two important patterns: the moon's **lunar cycle** and the seasons of the agricultural year.

At first, the Roman calendar had only ten months, each month beginning with a new moon. The calendar started in March with spring planting and ended in December with the planting of winter crops. What happened to the time in between? The early Romans didn't formally count this period because there was no work being done in the fields!

⋀ Early Romans recognized that the moon appears to slowly change shape from our point of view on Earth. It goes from a dark new moon to a bright full moon. Then back to a new moon again. This lunar cycle takes about 29.5 days. Ancient Romans used this cycle to develop an early calendar.

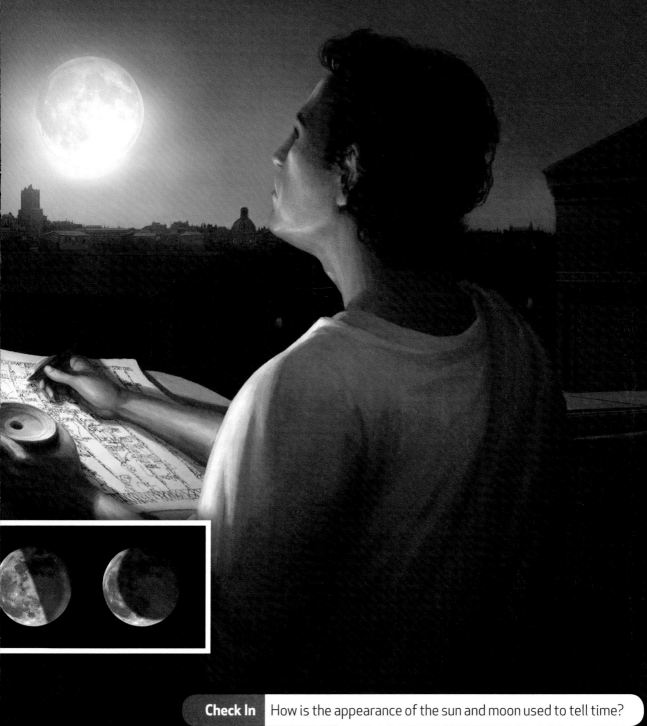

Check In How is the appearance of the sun and moon used to tell time?

Monsoon!

by Christopher Siegel

Much work needs to be done between seasons in Bangladesh. This farmer is plowing a rice paddy.

It's summer in Bangladesh, toward the end of the dry season. The weather is mostly hot and humid and the air feels heavy and sticky. It's uncomfortable to be outside in the heat and everyone wears loose clothing to try and stay cool under the hot sun. The ground is very dry and most of the vegetation has withered away because of the heat and dry conditions.

In many places the ground has baked into a hard, brown, crackled crust. There has been little to no rainfall for many weeks and dust covers the entire landscape. It seems that all living things in Bangladesh are in a holding pattern, waiting for the first gusts of wind and the first storm clouds to appear in the sky. The wind means one thing—the heavy rainfall of the wet season will soon be here. It is a relief from the dryness and dust that the people of Bangladesh and other parts of South Asia anticipate every year.

Each year Bangladesh has two distinct seasons: a wet season, usually from June to September, and a dry season, usually starting in October and ending sometime in May. This seasonally changing climate pattern is called **monsoon.** Monsoons are strong winds that change direction with the seasons. When the winds change direction, the weather also changes.

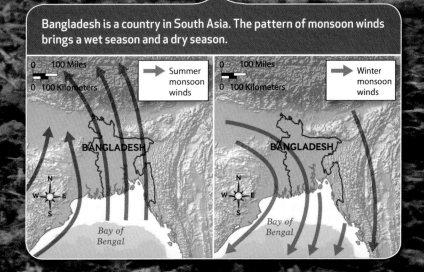

Bangladesh is a country in South Asia. The pattern of monsoon winds brings a wet season and a dry season.

0 100 Miles
0 100 Kilometers
Summer monsoon winds

0 100 Miles
0 100 Kilometers
Winter monsoon winds

BANGLADESH
N W E S
Bay of Bengal

BANGLADESH
N W E S
Bay of Bengal

Borsha: The Wet Season

JUNE TO SEPTEMBER

Usually in June, the blowing winds bring in the borsha, or wet season, in Bangladesh. Throughout most of the months of June through September, the rain is really in full swing. The rain keeps coming and coming, day after day, after day. Thankfully though, the rain isn't always a steady downpour throughout the entire day.

AVERAGE ANNUAL PRECIPITATION IN WORLD CITIES

DHAKA, BANGLADESH
185.4 centimeters (73.0 inches)

SEATTLE, WASHINGTON USA
96.5 cm (38 in)

CHICAGO, ILLINOIS USA
91.4 cm (36 in)

LONDON, ENGLAND
73.7 cm (29 in)

BEIJING, CHINA
63.5 cm (25 in)

Rather, days often start with a downpour, but usually by late afternoon the sky is clear and blue. The air outside, however, is still hot and, of course, it's still very humid because of all the water that begins to collect. In fact, it's difficult to keep dry during all these months of rainfall. The collecting rainwater quickly causes the rivers and streams to overflow. Floodwaters quickly overtake the land and everything on it.

People need to be especially careful during the rainy season. Flooding can cause loss of human life. Sometimes floodwaters sweep people off their feet. People can drown in the floodwater. Property can also be damaged. Homes are sometimes washed away. Utilities, such as electricity and drinking water supply lines, are often destroyed. Transportation also becomes very difficult due to flooded roads and railroad tracks. Many communities in Bangladesh and elsewhere become small islands, surrounded entirely by floodwater. It becomes difficult for people to leave such areas and for others to enter towns and villages.

Children jump puddles through a flooded field. Floodwaters quickly cover entire fields as the monsoon rains continue throughout the wet season.

Farmers clear weeds from a rice paddy. Crops and other plants quickly grow after the floodwaters recede.

Rabi: The Dry Season

OCTOBER TO MAY

Usually in October the winds begin to blow in a new direction. There is another sigh of relief from the people. This time it is because they know that these new gusts of wind are a sign that the rain will soon stop and the floodwaters will recede. People are tired of the mess from the flooding and the difficulty it causes. People want to begin to clean up and start a new season.

This new season is rabi, or the dry season, in Bangladesh. Like always, the weather is still warm but now it's at last dry. There is a lot of work to do while the land dries out. Work is needed to restore the damage from the previous floods. Utilities need to be fixed. Roads, railroads, and washed out bridges need to be rebuilt. Fields need to be planted with crops such as cotton and wheat.

All too soon the temperature will soar. Crops are planted, grow, ripen, and are then harvested. The ground will once again bake and the green landscape will turn brown. Then, soon enough the telltale wind will change direction again. The storm clouds will gather as they did months before and the borsha, the wet season, will come again. It is a pattern the people of Bangladesh know all too well.

Check In How does monsoon affect life in Bangladesh?

17

D-DAY!

HOW TIDES CHANGED HISTORY

by Rebecca L. Johnson

It was spring, 1944 during World War II. The Axis Powers, including German troops commanded by Nazi leader Adolph Hitler, had invaded Western Europe. France was under their control. The Allied Forces, including the United Kingdom, British Commonwealths, the United States, and the Soviet Union, were determined to defeat the Axis and Hitler's armies. They hoped to do this by launching an invasion of France. So what was their plan? It was to send troops across the English Channel. The Allies wanted to land thousands of soldiers on France's Normandy coast.

But there was one big problem. To guard against an invasion, the Germans had constructed wooden, steel, and cement obstacles on Normandy's beaches. This barrier of obstacles was designed to work with the **tide,** the recurring rise and fall of sea levels along the coast. At **high tide,** seawater would cover the beaches, hiding the obstacles. But high tide would also be the best time for Allied ships to land soldiers because they could get closer to shore. But if Allied ships arrived at high tide, they would certainly hit the hidden obstacles and sink.

What did the Allies do? Their military leaders decided to have their ships arrive at **low tide,** when the obstacles were exposed. Special teams would dynamite openings through the barrier, making it safe for the ships to approach the shore as the tide started to rise. For this daring plan to work, the Allied ships had to time their arrival to the minute!

German commander, Field Marshal Erwin Rommel, inspects the barriers at low tide.

Allied troops prepare for the D-Day Invasion.

Codenamed Operation Overlord, the final planning for the invasion began in late 1943. In preparation, the Allied commanders reviewed maps of the beaches and the waters of the English Channel the Allied troops would need to cross to begin the invasion. The allied invasion would set out from ports along England's southern coast and sail toward the heavily fortified German-controlled beaches in Normandy, France. But they had to decide what day and time would be best.

The timing of the low and high tides had to be exactly right. The pattern of the tides needed to be calculated to the second. Only at the precise moment of low tide would the obstacles covering the beach be exposed. Only at low tide could the invasion be successful. Otherwise troops would be lost and the mission a failure. To calculate the tides, the Allied commanders turned to scientists who studied the predictable movement of the ocean and its tides. One scientist was especially helpful.

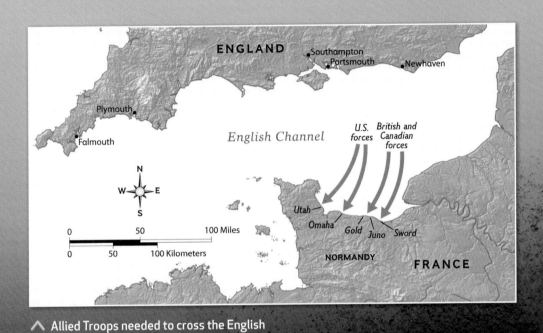

∧ Allied Troops needed to cross the English Channel. The Channel is an area of water between Great Britain and France.

The exact route each ship would travel across the Channel needed to be plotted.

Arthur Doodson

For this part of the mission, the Allied Forces turned to British scientist Arthur Doodson for help. At the time, Doodson was a world authority on tides. He worked at the Liverpool Tidal Institute, which had two mechanical tide-predicting machines. Doodson assured the Allied Forces that he could use the machines to figure out when low tide would occur along the Normandy coast and how quickly the tide would rise in the hours that were to follow.

Before Doodson could begin, he needed detailed information about the Normandy beaches. Their size and shape would affect the timing of the tides. In small boats, British special force teams sailed across the Channel. They conducted secret midnight missions along the French coast to gather the data that Doodson needed.

Using this information, Doodson made many calculations. Then he programmed the two tide-predicting machines and started running them. Brass gears spun and pulleys whirled. Working around the clock with his machines, Doodson produced tide predictions for the dates of the planned D-Day invasion.

Ships and blimps lined France's Normandy coast.

Doodson used this tide-predicting machine to calculate the tides.

HYDROGRAPHIC DEPARTMENT
ADMIRALTY
BATH

MOST URGENT
HOURLY HEIGHTS FOR POSITION Z
for 4 months commencing 1st April
1944.
Time zone   0 hours
Z_0 14.1 feet
M_2 272°   7.9'
S_2 317°   2.6'
K_2 ~~112°   0.3'~~
N_2 250°   1.6'
K_2 317°   0.7'
K_1 112°   0.3'
O_1 000°   0.2'
M_4 064°   0.6'
MS_4 146°   0.3'
M_6 200°   0.4'
SM_6 100°   0.2'
P_1 102°   0.1'

Send first
15 days as
soon as
possible.

9.10.43.

Handwritten notes detail the tides.

Shortly before dawn on June 6, 1944, more than 5,000 Allied ships reached the Normandy coast. The Germans didn't expect them and were largely unprepared for an attack. In fact, the German commander, Field Marshal Erwin Rommel, was so sure the Allied Forces wouldn't try to invade that he'd left the day before to visit his wife in Germany!

THE D-DAY INVASION TURNED THE TIDE OF WORLD WAR II.

The tide predictions made by Doodson and his big brass machines turned out to be very accurate. The Allied ships moved into position just after low tide. Demolition teams succeeded in blowing up wide openings through the barrier. As the tide rose, smaller boats carried tens of thousands of Allied soldiers to the beaches. The soldiers waded ashore and began fighting their way inland. The invasion of the German stronghold had begun!

By the end of the day, the Allied Forces had gained a strong foothold on the Normandy coast. It was a fierce battle and more than 9,000 Allied soldiers were killed or wounded. But overall, the D-Day invasion was a tremendous success. Soon after, more than 100,000 Allied soldiers began marching across Europe, with the mission of helping "turn the tide" of World War II and ultimately defeat Hitler and the Axis forces.

Allied soldiers make their way to the Normandy beaches.

Check In What steps were taken to make the D-Day invasion a success for the Allied Forces?

Read to find out about the predictable appearances of Halley's Comet.

Halley's Comet

by Rebecca L. Johnson

Halley's Comet has been observed throughout most of history. People have recorded its passing in different ways. But little was known about the comet until Edmund Halley applied the principles of mathematics and scientific discovery to determine the pattern of the comet's appearance over Earth.

Edmund Halley

This picture shows Halley's Comet in the night sky. It was taken in the Sonoran Desert in 1986.

Edmund Halley was very good at seeing patterns. English astronomer, meteorologist, and mathematician, Halley was the first person to describe the changing wind patterns that bring about the **monsoons** in India. But he is most known for figuring out another pattern. He determined that a comet people had been seeing periodically over the last few hundred years was actually the same comet. It seemed to be a comet with a distinctive pattern.

Halley himself only witnessed the comet once in his lifetime, in 1682. He was 25 years old at the time. But Halley never forgot about what he had witnessed that night in the dark sky above him.

A Pattern in the Sky

Twenty-five years later, Halley calculated that the comet had an elliptical, or egg-shaped, **orbit** within Earth's solar system. Its orbit takes the comet close to Earth as Earth travels around the sun. Halley also studied accounts of previous observations of comets or lights in the sky. He soon realized that some of these historical sightings were of the same comet he had seen. Using this information, he calculated that the comet's orbit carried it back near Earth every 75 or 76 years.

He also predicted—using the pattern he'd identified—that the comet would return in 1759. He was correct, although he didn't live to see the event.

Halley's Comet has two tails. These tails are like ribbons of traveling gases, dust, and other debris. The tails follow the nucleus and coma.

Halley's Comet consists of a solid nucleus, or core. A cloudy atmosphere surrounds the nucleus. This part is called the coma.

Halley's Comet is visible to the unaided eye when it passes close to the sun. We can see it from Earth because the gas and dust in its coma and tails reflect sunlight.

1531

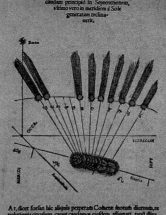

Drawings by Peter Apian

A German astronomer, Peter Apian, observed the comet in 1531. He reported that the comet's tail always stretched away from the sun. Apian created hand-drawn illustrations of his observations.

1607

Observations by Johannes Kepler

Johannes Kepler was a German mathematician and astronomer. He is best known for his study of how planets move. He recorded his observations of the comet in 1607. Kepler believed that comets moved in straight lines, although he thought planets moved in elliptical, or egg-shaped, orbits.

1682

Sightings in 1682

Although Halley saw the comet for himself in 1682, many other people recorded their observations, too. This artist engraving shows a comet with a long, golden tail. The art shows a positive interest toward seeing a comet in the night sky.

Recognizing the Pattern

Since Halley's day, historians, astronomers, and mathematicians have worked together to find records of sightings of the comet. Many date back thousands of years, well before Edmund Halley. As you can see, the appearance of what is now known as Halley's Comet has been a pattern that has been repeating for a long, long time!

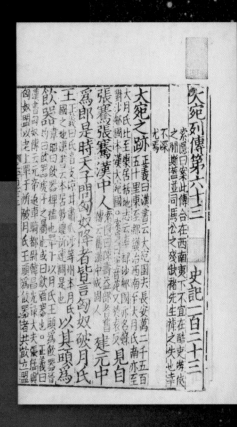

240 BC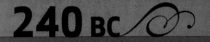

Records of the Grand Historian The first reliable sighting of Halley's Comet in the historical record is believed to be part of an ancient Chinese document. It is called the Records of the Grand Historian. The records note the observance of a bright object in the sky that matches the comet's description.

164 BC

Babylonian Clay Tablet
Inscribed on the tablet is a reference to a comet appearing in the night sky during the month of September. It is described as appearing in the east and moving north.

87 BC

Stamped Coin The Armenian king Tigranes the Great may have seen the comet during this year. Soon after, he had coins stamped with his likeness wearing a crown topped with a star with a curved tail.

1066 AD

Bayeux Tapestry The comet arrived in the year that William, Duke of Normandy, gained control of England. An image of the comet was woven into the upper right portion of the Bayeux Tapestry. The tapestry is an immensely long embroidered cloth that depicts more than 50 scenes of the invasion.

↑ Halley's Comet

Thanks to the power of patterns and mathematics, we know Haley's Comet will be visible from Earth about every 75-76 years. The next time will be about 2061. How old will you be?

Check In Calculate which year Halley's Comet will be visible after 2061.

Discuss

1. "Passage of Time" describes how the sun and moon's apparent movement over Earth have been used to chart the passing of time since ancient times. Find out other ways the sun and moon's apparent movement are still used today.

2. "Monsoon" describes how climate changes in Bangldesh. How is this similar or different from where you live?

3. The D-Day selection describes how tides impacted World War II. Identify other events that have been influenced by tides.

4. Halley's Comet can be seen from Earth every 75–76 years. Calculate how old you will be when you could see it?

5. What are some other patterns in Earth and space that interest you? What else do you wonder about these patterns?